DOWNTON ABBEY

ORIGINAL MUSIC FROM THE TELEVISION SERIES

WISE PUBLICATIONS
part of The Music Sales Group
London / New York / Paris / Sydney / Copenhagen / Berlin / Madrid / Hong Kong / Tokyo

Published by
Wise Publications
14-15 Berners Street, London W1T 3LJ, UK.

Exclusive Distributors:
Music Sales Limited
Distribution Centre, Newmarket Road,
Bury St Edmunds, Suffolk IP33 3YB, UK.
Music Sales Pty Limited
20 Resolution Drive, Caringbah, NSW 2229, Australia.

Order No. AM1004366
ISBN: 978-1-78038-408-5
This book © Copyright 2011 Wise Publications,
a division of Music Sales Limited.

Edited by Jenni Norey.
Arranged by Jeremy Birchall & Christopher Hussey.
Arrangements and engravings
supplied by Camden Music Services.

Printed in the EU.

Downton Abbey - The Suite

Music by John Lunn

Allegro con spirito ♩ = 165

Love And The Hunter

Music by John Lunn

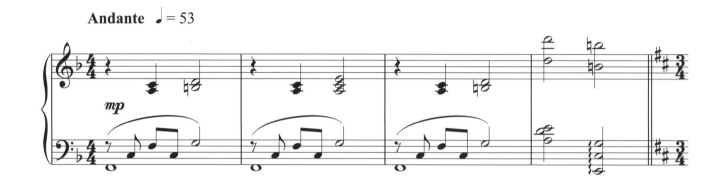

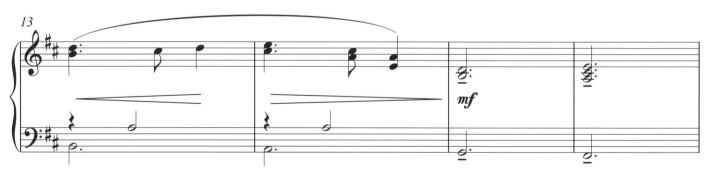

Poco più mosso ♩ = 170

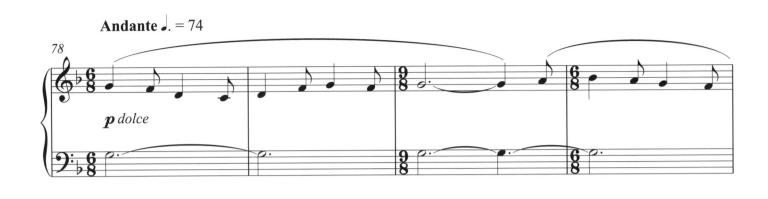

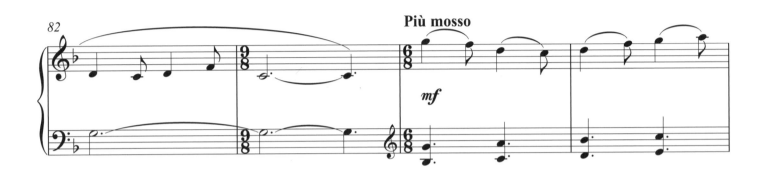

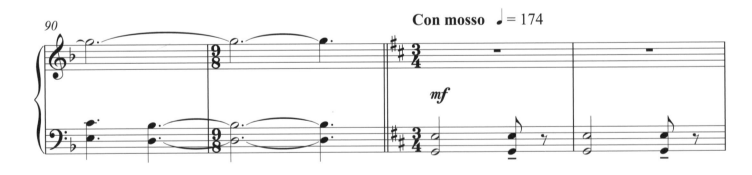

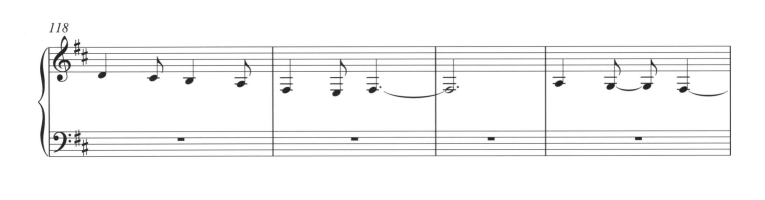

Emancipation

Music by John Lunn

Allegro moderato ♩ = 149

Lento ♩ = 62

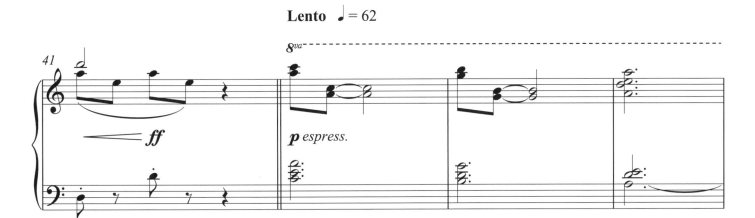

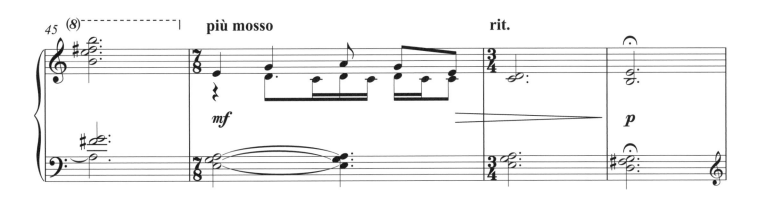

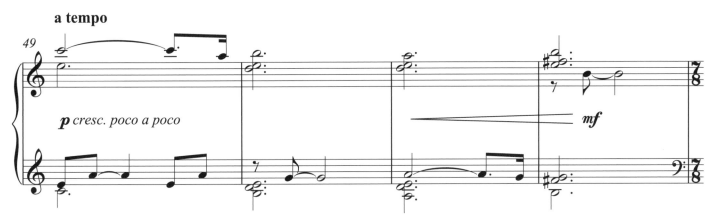

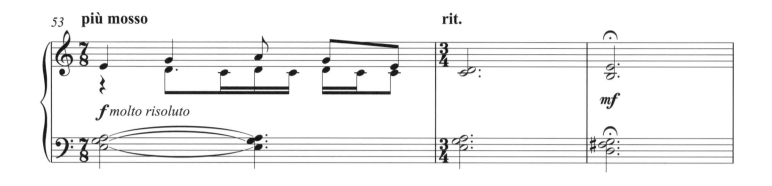

Story Of My Life

Music by John Lunn

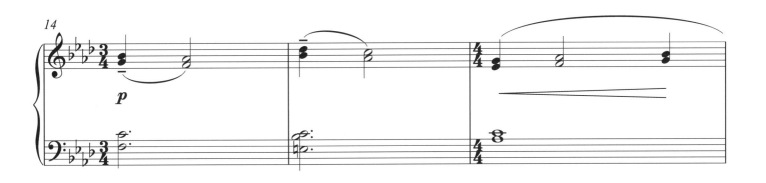

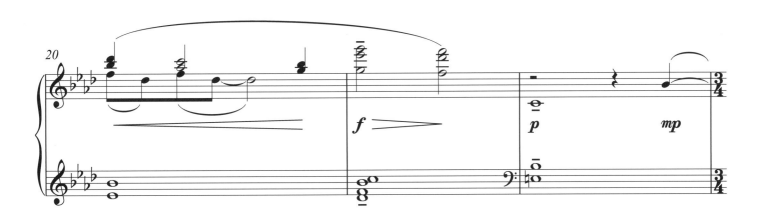

Fashion

Music by John Lunn

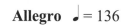

29

Damaged

Music by John Lunn

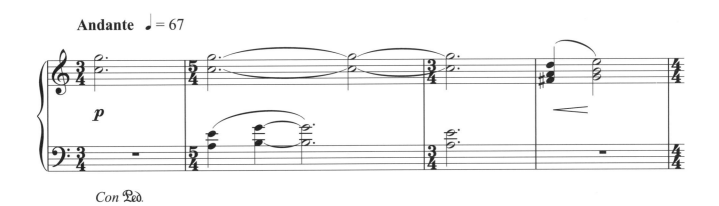

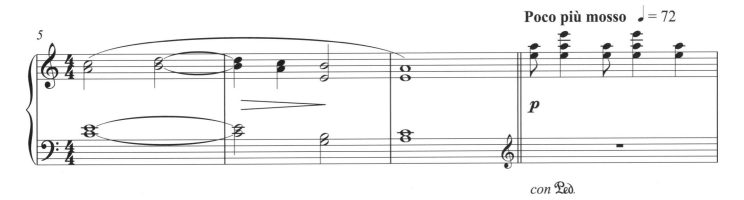

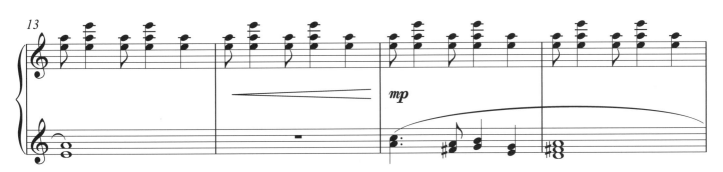

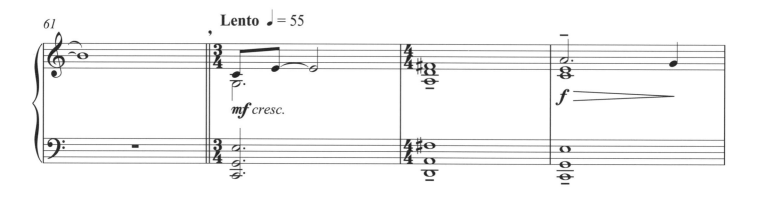

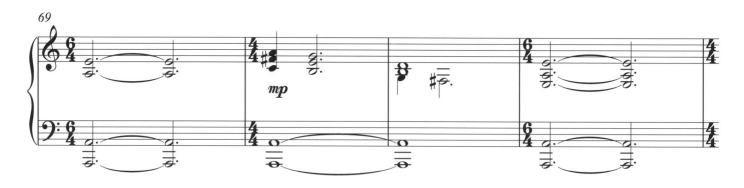

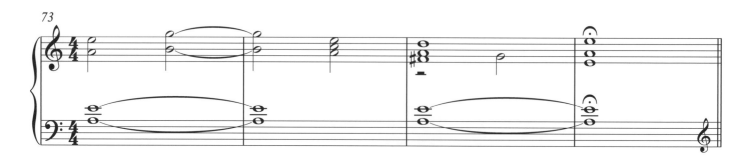

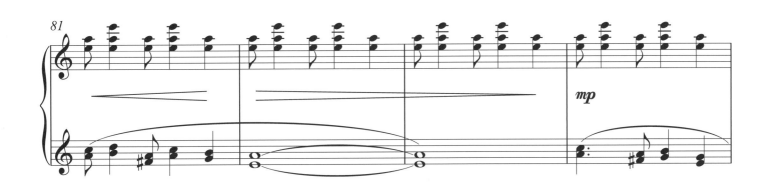

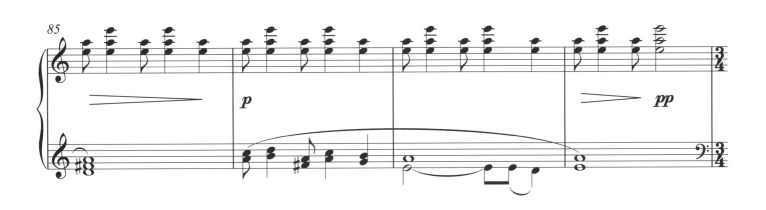

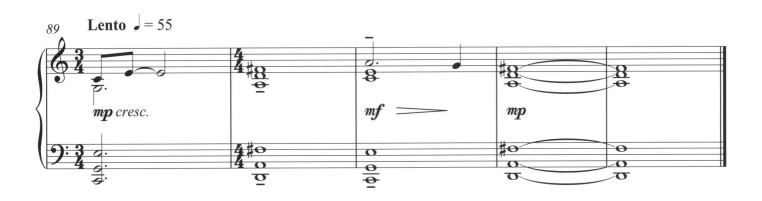

Preparation

Music by John Lunn

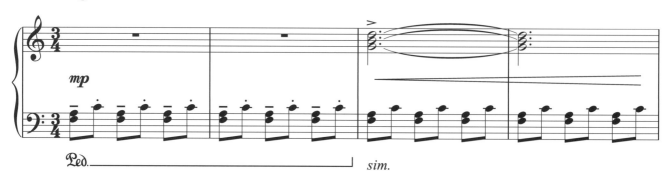

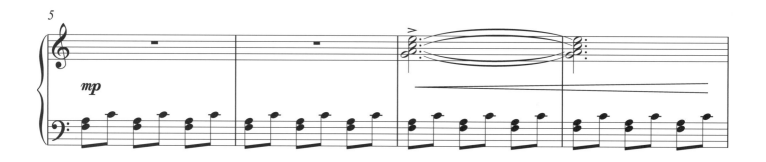

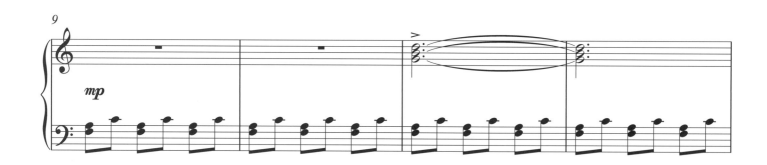

sim.

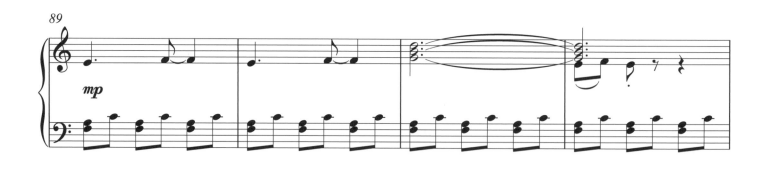

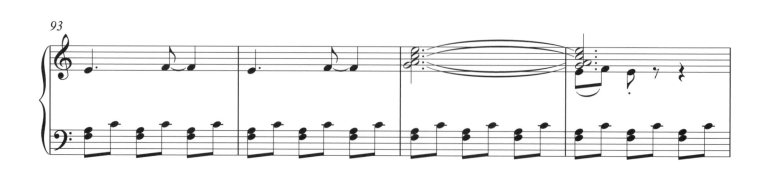

43

Such Good Luck

Music by John Lunn

Moderato ♩ = 80

Meno mosso

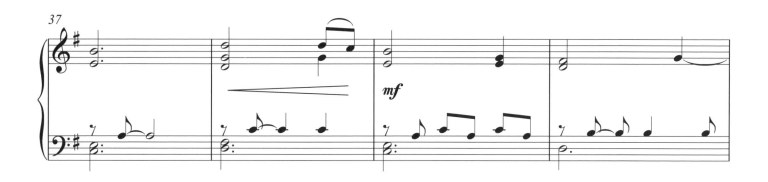

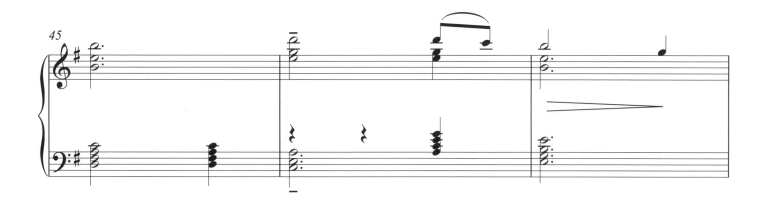

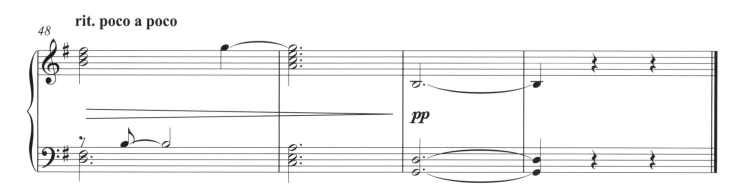

Us And Them

Music by John Lunn

Allegro scherzando ♩ = 180

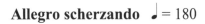

Violet

Music by John Lunn

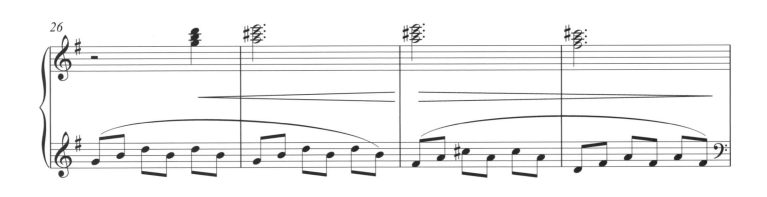

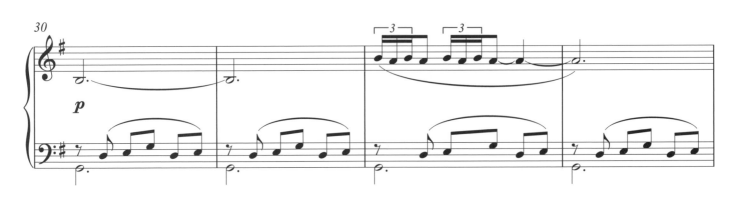

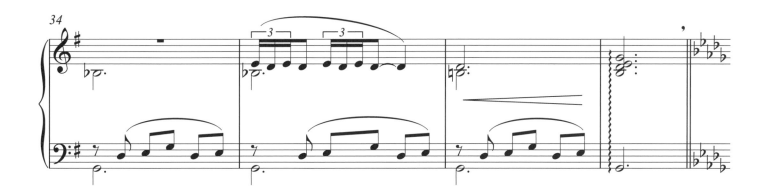

Meno mosso ♩ = 80

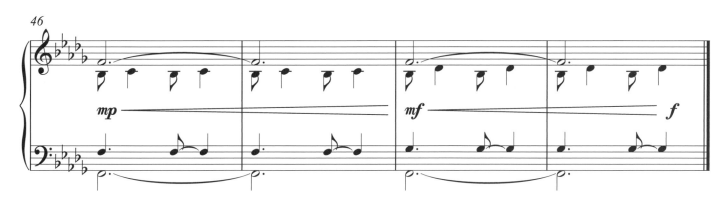

A Drive

Music by John Lunn

Allegro energico ♩ = 164

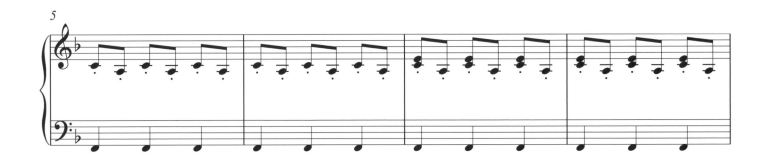

An Ideal Marriage

Music by John Lunn

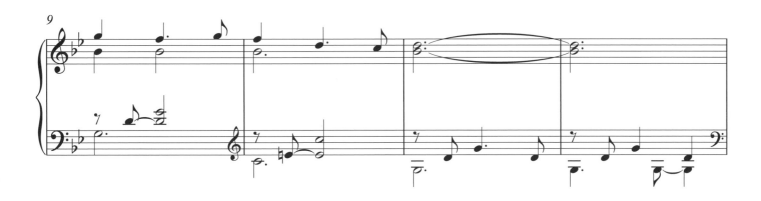

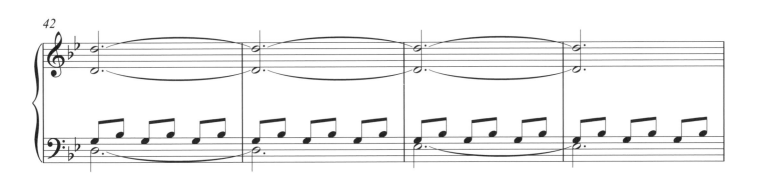

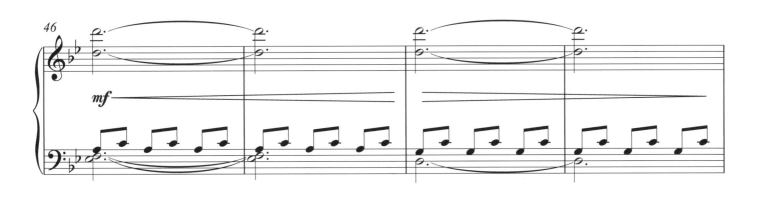

poco rit.   **A tempo**

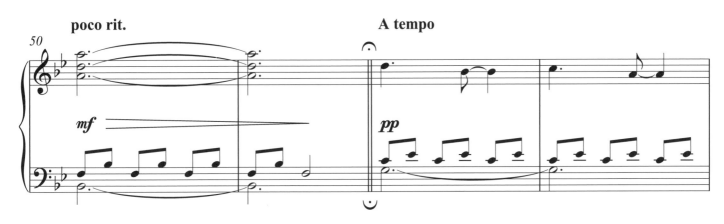

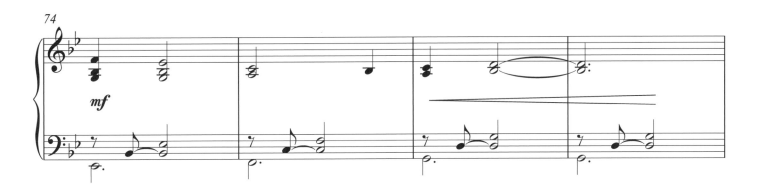

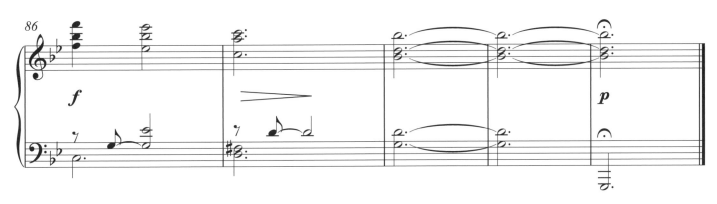

Telegram

Music by John Lunn

Allegro ♩ = 160

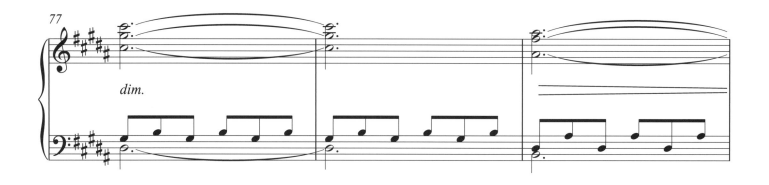

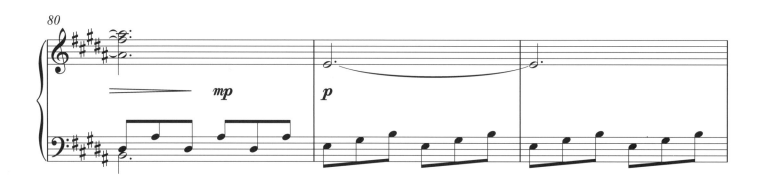

Deception

Music by John Lunn

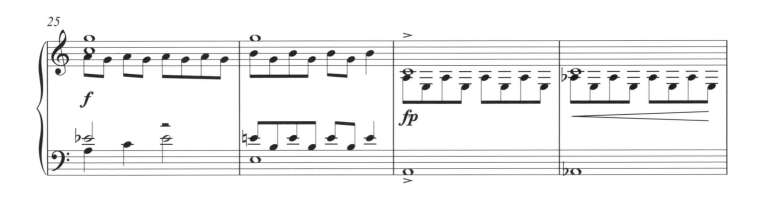

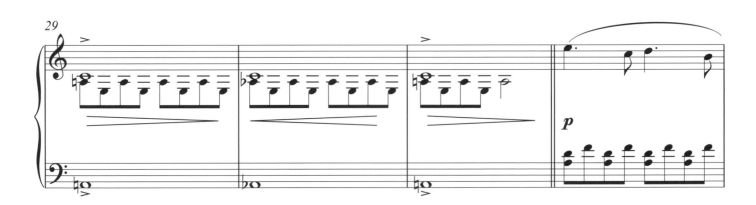

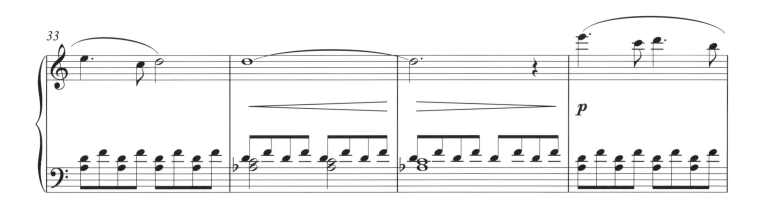

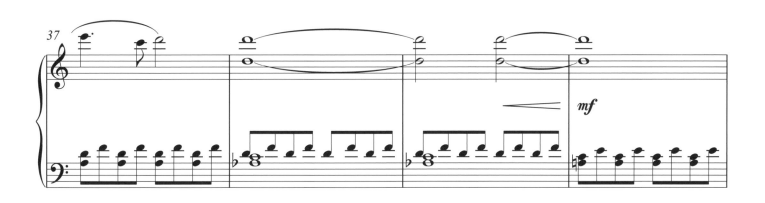

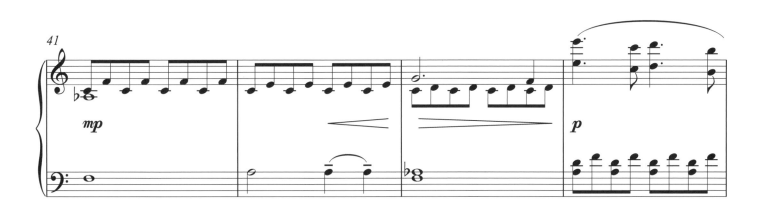

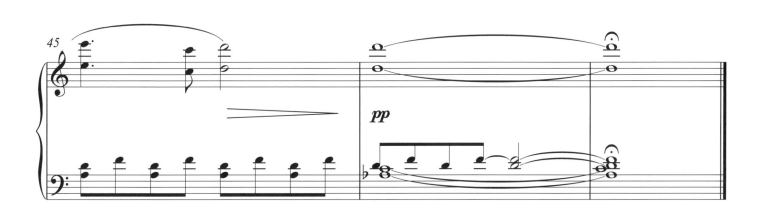

Titanic

Music by John Lunn

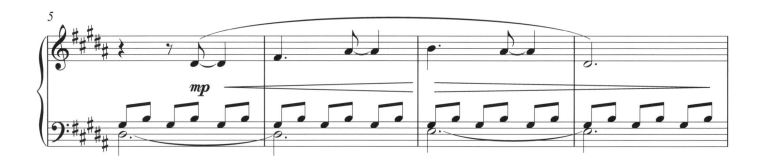

A Song And A Dance

Music by John Lunn

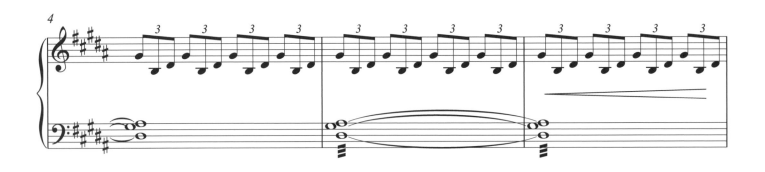

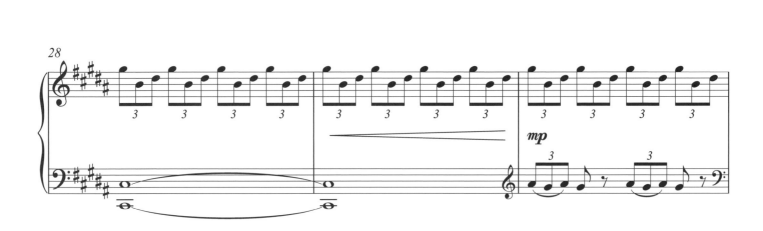

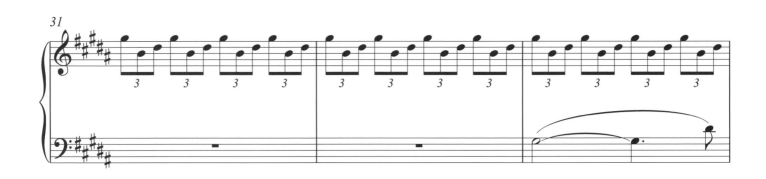

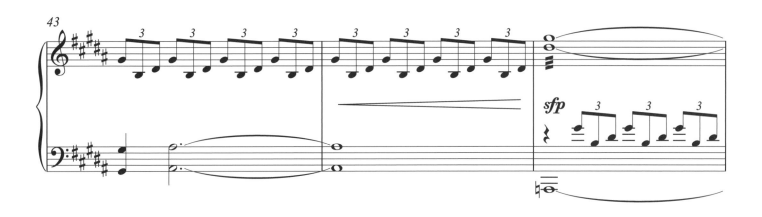

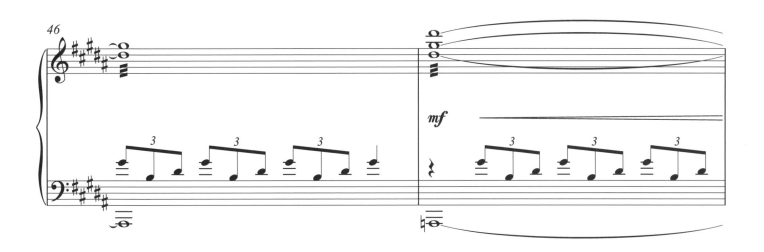

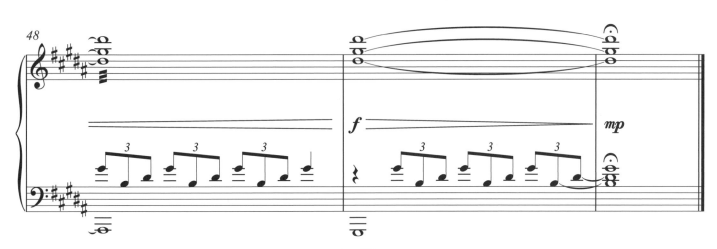

Did I Make The Most Of Loving You?

Words by Don Black
Music by John Lunn

Con moto ♩ = 167

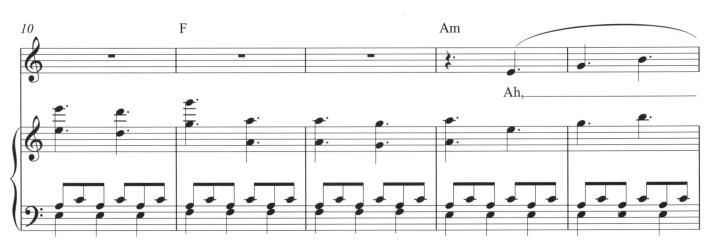

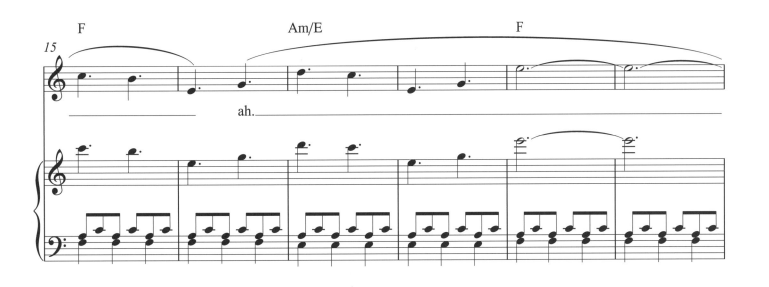

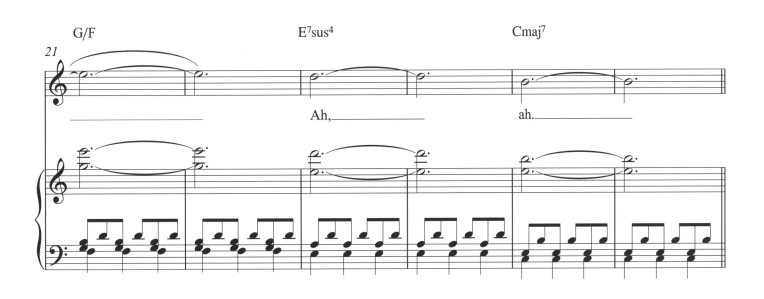

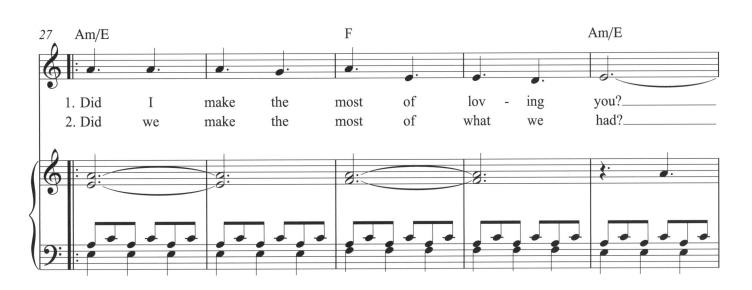

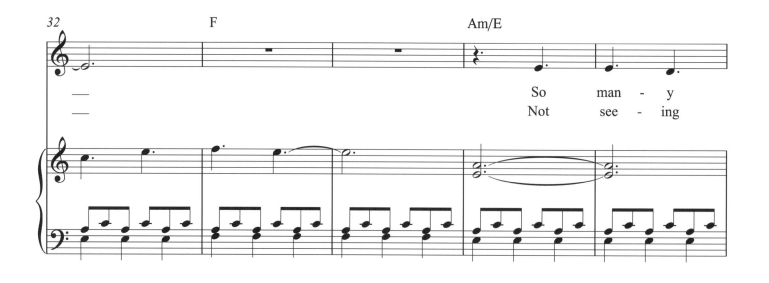

So man - y
Not see - ing

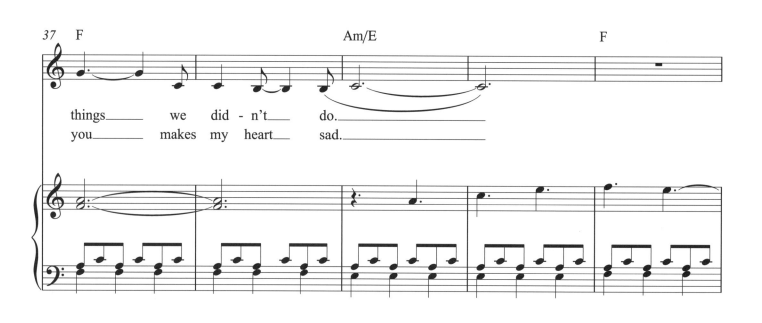

things_____ we did - n't___ do._____
you_____ makes my heart___ sad._____

Did I give you all my heart could__
Did we make the all most of sum - mer__

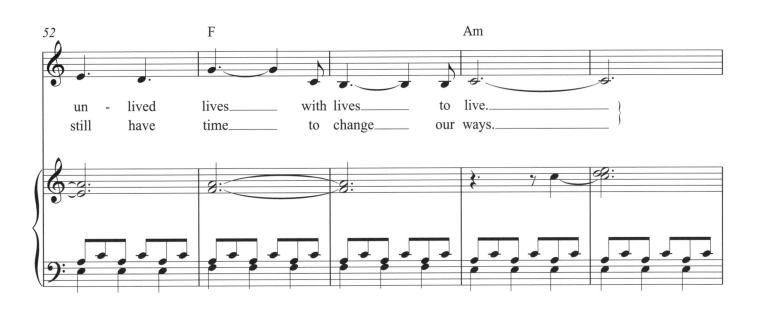

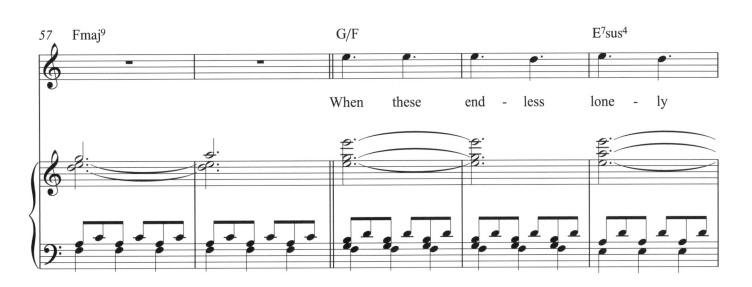

3. Did those ten-der words stay in my head?

So man-y

things were left un-said.

Did I give you all my heart could

456789